Seasons of Love
Donni & George Betts

Celestial Arts ● *Berkeley, California*

CELESTIAL ARTS PUBLISHING
P.O. Box 7327
Berkeley, California 94707

Cover & interior design by Ken Scott
Typography by Ann Flanagan

Library of Congress Cataloging-in-Publication Data

Betts, Donni.
    Seasons of love.
    I. Betts, George.   II. Title.
PS3552.E85S4   1986   811'. 54   86-11733
ISBN 0-89087-477-8

Manufactured in the United States of America

1 2 3 4 5 — 91 90 89 88 87

Winter came to our love,
and we returned to the warmth
and security of each other,
comfortable in the knowledge
that together,
with patience and tolerance
we could weather any storm.
Our love has grown
from openness, honesty
and devotion to each other
as well as our selves,
and we are strong.

Spring has come again,
and with it
the sense of newness,
as we continue to nurture
and cultivate the love
that blossomed long ago.

With each season,
each year,
the roots of our love
will deepen
and we will continue
growing together...

○

Spring

"Our love is the vehicle that will carry us into tomorrow."

Several years have passed since we met. Our lives have changed dramatically. We are stronger, more secure with each other and more secure with our selves. We have journeyed into unknown lands, and back to the familiar, gaining insight with each new step. I appreciate today, for we are loving, in love and thoroughly involved with life. We are fully alive...

But where did we begin? How did we get to this place of acceptance and understanding?

I want to take time to understand our ever-changing life, our ever-searching day-to-day living, our belief in love, in life and in ourselves. I want to look back, to reflect, to try to grasp an understanding of the many seasons of our love...

Seasons of Love

It began with a look,
conveying a message
*   we weren't yet ready*
*   to put into words.*
Through our eyes,
*   our expressions,*
we began to form a language
of friendship,
a basis for the love we were
not yet ready to share.
Silently
our friendship grew,
our communication expanded.
Words gained new meaning
as the language of love evolved
and we became more sure of ourselves
in this new, exciting adventure.
And now, when we share a special look
I remember the first days,
*   the days of that special friendship,*
and I'm thankful.
For now, after all this time
*   you are still my friend . . .*

How can we be lovers
if we aren't even friends?
Relationships develop so fast.
Push — — no time for tomorrow.
Accomplish everything today.
But wait,
please slow down,
let me show you
what I am,
where I am, and
where I am going.

I want my freedom
but I also want you.
Can I have both?
Are you different?
Will you give me new freedom to enjoy
Those things I would miss if you were gone?

Do I love you
  for what you are
  or what you give to me?
I hope it's just for
  what you are.
I'd like to think that
  you can be you
    and be free
      to go your way;
that there's nothing here
    to hold you to me
    but the gentle breeze
      that moves softly
        between our souls,
        and speaks the things
          our words could never express...

It isn't always easy
to say what's in my heart.

Sometimes I feel things that seem
too personal to share,
or that might be hurtful
and I want to keep them to myself.

But I have learned
those are the times
it's most important to speak up,
so I don't create walls that keep you out.

Thank you for making it safe
to say what I feel.

*Being alike
has brought us
together.
Being different
will help us
to grow.*

M*y world*
  and my heart
are open to you.
Be gentle,
take what you need,
  give what you can
for our time together
can enhance our lives.

I can not always be
    beautiful
       and unselfish.
You can not always be
    kind
       and understanding.
We are both human.
We have to be real.

The heart is not touched
    continually,
but it is those precious times
that make everything
    in our lives
       worthwhile…

S e a s o n s   o f   L o v e

What was I like before I met you?

Was I growing, searching,
looking for answers through people
*   and experiences?*
Yes.
What am I like now that I have found you?
I am still growing, searching,
looking for answers through people
*   and experiences . . .*
How have you affected my life?
You have helped me to be
*   more secure within myself,*
*   more aware of the feelings of others,*
*   more honest and spontaneous*
*   in my experiences,*
*   more loving and accepting.*
You have helped me to be more of what I am
*   capable of becoming.*
I have grown because of you,
*   your love for me,*
*   and the security you have helped me to*
*   develop.*
I am richer because of you . . .

○

*H*ow wonderful to finally have found you.
For so long I searched,
looking for the special one
　　　to share my life with,
someone who would accept
　　　and love me as I am,
　　　　and yet provide the freedom and encouragement
　　　　　for me to outgrow my self-limitations.
I longed for someone to admire, to love,
　　　　someone who was striving to be
　　　　　the best they could be.
Yet somehow
　　　each relationship fell short
and I became more sure
there would never be anyone
　　　　with whom I could build a love
　　　　　and a life.

Finally I stopped searching
and began to accept that
　　　my life might be complete
without having someone to share.
I began building friendships
　　　rather than creating loves,

and one of my friends
              was you.

Our admiration grew,
     nurtured by time
and love began to blossom,
          not from a need,
          but from a desire to be together.
And now,
          many years later
          I am thankful
we both stopped searching
and found each other...

Summer

"To communicate with you I must first know myself"

We have achieved a unique balance in our relationship. You are strong, dynamic, outgoing, I am quiet, gentle, a listener. We both love people and when we are together our giving is multiplied by the balance in our personalities.

It has not always been easy. There has been conflict, struggle, as of course there must always be in a vital, changing, evolving relationship. But we see the difficult moments as opportunities for taking risks, for gaining a new understanding of ourselves and each other; a chance to go beyond our present circumstance.

We use our conflicts as an opportunity to communicate, and communication is the key to the balance in our life together.

You say you love me,

    that you accept me,

but why do you frown when I act differently?

Can't you accept the different sides of me?

I must change as I live.

Don't ask me to sacrifice my growth

    to meet your expectations.

        I am what I am.

If you do love me, you'll understand.

○

What now?
We've talked for hours
but nothing has been said.

We care so deeply
but our feelings are lost
when we desperately try
to find each other.

You avoid my glances.
I talk about nothing...
Silence...
Finally the waiter announces
that it's time to close.

For moments our eyes meet
and I'm somewhat refreshed,
because even though it's painful
we'll try again.

Love is so hard to understand,
at times.

Frustration...
  incompletion...
Why?
  You helped create it
    and now you're asleep,
      safe,
and I feel alone.
  What do I do with it?

I can't talk
  with no one to listen.
Maybe you're right...
  Maybe sleep is the answer
  for those who can...
      I can't.

How can people
who love each other
so much
cause such hurt
for each other?

Why do I say things
that hurt you?
Why do you get
so upset?
Why do we always
have to withdraw?
Can't you see I'm
willing to let go of
the hurt feelings
and be close?

Don't you know that
all I really want
is to love you?

○

Admitting I was wrong
is the hardest thing I have done.
I was so sure of myself
and I knew I had
to stand up to you.

But you were strong
and now I understand . . .

Thank you for believing
in yourself
and for being
honest with me . . .

I have grown . . .

The time for honesty has come.

I can no longer hide behind
excuses and avoidance.

I must finally accept the reality
of my feelings
and face the consquences
of owning them.

Because, painful as it may be,
the truth
hurts much less
than trying to hide from it.

○

*When I withdraw,
when I become defensive,
when I act as if I don't care.*

*These are the times
I need you most.*

Loving you is not always easy
but if it were

I probably wouldn't.

If I hurt you,
it's not intentionally.
If you feel insecure with me
it's not because I want it that way.
If I neglect to show you
how much I appreciate you,
it's from a lack of awareness.
I try to do the best I can
but sometimes, in my bumbling,
imperfect way,
I mess things up.
Can you hear me?

To hear you
I must first listen to my own inner voice.
I must understand my needs,
my problems,
   my strengths and weaknesses.
I hear your words,
but not always your message.
My past gets in my way
   and I interpret what I hear
according to old experiences
even though they don't apply to
   our relationship.
I misunderstand you,
   and hurt follows.
I think you don't like part of me.
When will I be able to listen
   only to your message
   without putting a different meaning
      to your words?

I was angry with you
          for changing,
for not being what you've
               always been,
          what I've needed you to be.

I couldn't accept
that you were not the same
          reliable person
          I've always counted on.

I know we can't recapture
the past,
               but can we go on,
                    create something new
from the change in our relationship?

It frightens me,
for I know it means that
          I must change too.
Is it worth it?
Am I willing to let go
          of our old relationship,
               to build something new
               with what we now have?

○   *35*

Please be with me
    when I cry,
        when I'm down,
            when I'm hurting.
I know it's hard for you,
    that you get tired of it,
        but that's what
            loving is about...
    sharing the hard times
        as well as the good times.
I need you now
    more than ever.
And you know
    I'll be with you
        when it's your turn to cry.

We're doing it once again...
solving our problems,
finishing our conflicts
and bringing closure to our lives.

Tomorrow
we might have
to begin once again,
but for today
we have brought peace
into our lives
and once again
we are able to relax
and appreciate what it means
to truly care...

I've seen people and relationships
destroyed by distrust and jealousy.

I'm so thankful that the love we share
is built on trust
        and joy for each other's accomplishments.

Rather than tearing each other down,
        or fighting such destructive feelings,
we are free to enjoy each other,
        confident that the support
                we give one another
will in due time
        be returned.

Fall

*"What a wonderful task
we have,
to work at living together,
keeping love alive…"*

*Our love has withstood the test of time and
we are coming to a new understanding of what
"together" can mean.*

*In the beginning I thought being together
meant sharing everything in our lives; that being
apart would mean losing some of the closeness we
treasure so much.*

*But as we have grown and become more
secure, both within ourselves and our relationship,
we have loosened our grasp and found that,
through time, it is the only way to hold on to
something as precious as our love.*

*"Together" can mean being secure enough in
our love to travel half-a-world away, alone. It can
also mean struggling with self-doubts, knowing we
will be supportive as we learn to resolve personal
conflicts. Being together is knowing, finally, that
our relationship can survive many difficulties and
emerge stronger because we have learned once
again to work together, to listen, to understand.*

Seasons of Love

It's Autumn again.
A year has passed
but the falling leaves
relive the memories
of our autumn.

We shared the
melting of the snow,
 the warming of the sun,
but then the leaves
 began to fall,
 and now I realize
that a tree must give
 and at times, become empty
before it is able to grow and give again,
and so it is with me.

At times I must leave you
and go deep inside
where I can explore
the mysteries of my mind,
of my being.

I must settle things
with myself . . .

then,
I am able to travel
back to you
and we can continue together
but at times,
I must leave you.

Seasons of Love

The time has come for introspection.
I need to look at my life,
to find a direction.
Where am I going?
What do I want my life
to say about me?
The choices are mine.
My life will be what I make it.
There are so many directions.
The options are limitless.
I feel overwhelmed.
What if I make some wrong choices?
What if I do something I'll regret?
And yet I must remember
there is never any assurance
that life will be perfect.
But there is one thing
of which I can be certain...
I will always have ME.
My strength lies within,
and knowing that
is all the guarantee I will ever have
or truly need...

*A*t times I need to wander
to distant lands and new experiences,
but life would not be complete
without the memory of home
and the ones I love.

I returned today
and found our home
warm and alive.
I'm happy to be here with you.

Being far away from you,
I think of you often,
but it is not an empty feeling.
It is a feeling
of appreciation.
I remember the uniqueness
of your expressions,
the depth
of your loving,
and the joy and laughter
you bring to my world.
And through my memories of you,
I am never alone.

In our relationship
we have discovered
how much we have to strive
 for our freedom…
not freedom from each other
 but freedom with each other,
to be what we truly are
 deep inside
and to know it's okay
 to be
 whatever that may be.

*Half of loving is
knowing when
to let go.*

Seasons of Love

I know you
       almost
as well as
       I know me.

I have learned
       your moods,
       your expressions,
your ability to give
              and receive,
and the way you strive
to be...

Your past
       holds both joy
              and sorrow
              and your future
                     is becoming brighter
       for you are developing
                            you.

I smile silently
       as you continue to grow...

Seasons of Love

For as long as we've known each other
I've never really told you
how I feel about you,
and I want you to know
what an important part of my life
you are.

A friendship like ours
is rare,
a chance for two people
to share their everyday thoughts
and deepest feelings
without feeling self-conscious
or inadequate.

No matter how long
we've been apart
my thoughts turn often
to you,
and I smile,
knowing that the next time
I see you
our friendship will have grown richer.
for we are both continually
enriching our own lives,
bringing a new dimension
to what we share.

○

The essence of me.
What does it mean?
How do I fit what I am
    with who you are?
How can we mold ourselves
into a twosome who can live together
    in harmony,
        striving for the same things . . .
Growth, happiness.
This must be the most difficult task in life . . .
to make a relationship work,
    to give it meaning, substance;
to find fulfillment together,
and yet manage, at the same time,
to develop the uniqueness of ourselves
    as individuals.
What a wonderful task we have,
to work at living together,
    keeping love alive . . .

In the gentle stillness of the night
    I sit alone
        and reflect on the many facets
    of our life together.

You bring out the best in me,
always encouraging me to grow,
    to reach just a little farther,
        to stretch just a little more.

You always seem to want what is
    truly best for me,
even if it isn't exactly what you would choose.

Your unselfish, giving nature
has opened my heart
    to a new way of sharing
and I can only hope
    that in my own way,
I bring out the best in you . . .

○

Do you remember the
"touching" moments
of your life,
those small but significant times
that have helped you to be
who you are now?
Last night I thought
of the touching moments
and began to explore my past.

There was the excitement
of being told
"You're beautiful, I love you."
There was the sorrow
of saying goodbye
to a true love
and knowing that love would never
come my way again.
There was the sorrow of death
and the search to understand.
There were the moments
of being alone,
when I began to learn
about myself inside.

There was the feeling
of self-acceptance,
and the excitement of reaching out
and finding others to love.

There was the satisfaction
of knowing that I am
changing and growing.
And now there is excitement
for today and
tomorrow...
I am open,
I am loved,
but most important,
I am alive.
My life has just begun...

Winter

Seasons of Love

"For now, after all this time you are still my friend..."

*Our love has changed. The newness is gone
and we are no longer living in a world of romance.
Our love will never be the same, but I feel no sad-
ness for our love has grown and we are stronger.
Although the newness is gone we now have a
deeper understanding, appreciation and respect
for each other as individuals.*

*Through our commitment we have developed
the security necessary to be ourselves, to take risks,
to be vulnerable.*

*We know the strengths, the weaknesses, the
goals and the dreams. We have experienced the
joys, the sorrows, the moments of anger and con-
flict, the times of tenderness and love. And through
it all we are renewed, ready for tomorrow, ready
to strengthen our love even beyond what it is today.
Our love has changed...*

Do you still remember...
   The day we first met?
      The first time
         we shared silently?
      The first walk
         through the park?
      The awkwardness
of opening up?
The first time we made love?
      The joy we shared
         as we discovered
      who we are,
            together?

So many things have faded from me
but not you, nor our memories.
They are so vivid,
            real,
as if they had happened yesterday.

Do you still remember...

It's funny . . .
people talk about falling in love.
But I didn't fall in love
                    with you.
I'm growing in love with you.

Our love is self-renewing
for we provide ourselves
with new experiences,
            healthy friends,
                exciting adventures
                    and time to enjoy
the beauties and pleasures
of life.
We are not stagnant . . .
Our love is forever
                changing . . .

○

I brought you flowers today,
for the first time in many months.

Our pace has been so fast
that we haven't
taken time
    for ourselves.

We give so much to others.
Our world is rich and full.
We have built a world
    of security and love
with our friends and ourselves,
but through our journey
we haven't taken time
    for us...
And this is why I gave you
    flowers today,
a symbol of our love.

As you enjoy your gift
take time to reflect.
These flowers represent
    our special moments.
Let us stop
    our involved pace
                if only for
moments,
    to take time
    to reflect,
        to appreciate,
and to realize that
    we are living a love
    that many people
            only dream about...

S e a s o n s   o f   L o v e

I find I hardly know this person
I've been living with for so long.
Lately we've grown,
    not apart,
        but in different directions.
I feel I don't know what happens
    in your daily life,
the forces that motivate you,
    the events that stir your emotions.
One thing I do know:
I find you intriguing
    exciting
        and most lovable.
A wonderful, vulnerable
and yet strong person.
I feel as though we're starting over,
    fresh,
        with renewed love
and interest in each other.

S e a s o n s   o f   L o v e

*Y*ou're sitting next to me,
  half a world away,
      lost in your own thoughts . . .
  I could feel lonely,
              left out,
          threatened.
  But I don't.
  I understand your need
          to be alone,
  although we are together.
  And this is the essence
          of our life together.
  For at times
          we need to create
              a space
  in which to reflect,
          to expand our thoughts
              in a way
  which is impossible
  if we cling too closely.
  But no matter how far apart
      we travel
  we remain together in our hearts.

*Between
appointments,
people,
schedules
and deadlines
I have had
the time
to realize
how
much
I love
and need you...
Tonight I'll bring
you flowers
and a bottle
of wine...
But before dinner,
please take
the phone
     off the hook...*

Funny, I never realized
how silent our home is
when you're away.

But even in the quiet
I feel
the comfort
of your presence.

Your gentleness will carry
me to sleep tonight
as it has every night.

Good night . . .
Sleep well . . .

Nighttime,
Silence.
We are alone,
This time belongs to us
  as no other does.

Our bodies
  touching,
 our voices
  silent,
 our hearts
  together, peaceful,
For a few hours
the world consists
  of you and me.

Morning comes
  and we slowly make our way
   back into the world
   of telephones
   and other people.
But it's all right
  because we always
   have
    our time.
The night belongs
    to us.

For us,
love is more
than saying hello
    and later, goodbye.
Our love did not begin
    just to end.
We have built a love
    different from any
      we have ever experienced
      before,
and the only thought
    we have about tomorrow
      is a continuation
      of today.

We have traveled
    through loneliness
    and sadness
to our place
    of understanding,
      our place of beauty
where we can continue
growing...
      together.

Why are we different from other couples?
So many relationships wither
but ours thrives on the sunshine,
    survives the storms
       and continues to grow
         stronger.

We are different
    for we have learned
      to let go,
        to communicate,
    to accept the differences,
to allow each other to be . . .

Our needs are being met.

I don't worry about tomorrow
    for we have learned to live today
to its fullest . . .

How fortunate we are to have each other . . .

We love each other.

Our love has
endured and has grown . . .
We will always face problems . . .
We will have conflicts,
misunderstandings
and discomfort . . .

but we have the ability
to communicate,
to strive for solutions,
to find new avenues of growth . . .

We love each other . . .
Our love is the vehicle
that will carry us into
tomorrow . . .

I'm waiting
for spring to arrive.
For newness,
        green
            freshness
        to burst into our lives
and banish the heavy,
        cloud-days of winter.

Already I can feel
the sunshine
        brought by blooming
            daffodils.
        The first perfumed hint
        of new-mown grass
and the sense of endless freedom
        that warm, cloudless
            days promise.

The sun is hidden now
behind a blanket
        of heavy white flakes
and yet I feel
        the airiness of spring
            welling inside me,
            warming me already.
It won't be long now . . .

○   77

We've been together
for many years now
    and the more I know you,
        the things that make you laugh,
          your most vulnerable places,
            the many ways you've grown...
The more I love you.

It's so easy to love
    in the beginning.
In the Springtime of love
    everything is new, fresh,
        exhilarating.
We've weathered the summer storms of conflict,
    working out our differences.
There will no doubt be more storms,
    but we'll survive them,
secure in the knowledge that our love
is deeply anchored in each other's hearts.

And we'll continue to love,
    to discover new seasons.
The more I know you...
    The more I love you.

ALSO BY GEORGE BETTS...

Visions of You presents a distinctly loving vision of the world in terms that are clear and accessible to every reader. This is the book that burst upon the horizon of bestselling poetry in the 1970s, and George has brought his modern, mature experience to bear on this updated, revised edition of that much-loved book.

Available at your local bookstore, or by direct mail order from the publisher. Send $5.95 (plus 75¢ for Fourth Class mail or $2.25 for UPS delivery; California residents please add 6.5% state sales tax) to: CELESTIAL ARTS PUBLISHING, P.O. Box 7327, Berkeley, California 94707.

A WORD FROM THE PUBLISHER...

CELESTIAL ARTS is the publisher of many fine books in the areas of personal growth, spirituality, and gourmet cookery. For a copy of our free catalog, please write to us at the address above or phone (415) 524-1801.